My Book of Prayers

by Helen Gompertz
illustrated by Linda Birch

Contents

SCRIPTURE UNION PUBLISHING

London   Sydney   Cape Town

© Scripture Union 1985
First Published 1985
Reprinted 1987, 1989, 1991, 1992, 1997

Published in the UK by
Scripture Union, 207-209 Queensway, Bletchley,
Milton Keynes, Buckinghamshire MK2 2EB
Distributed in Southern Africa by
SUPA, 83 Camp Ground Road, Rondebosch 7700

ISBN 0 85421 998 6

Phototypeset by Wyvern Typesetting Limited, Bristol
Made and printed in Great Britain by Ebenezer Baylis
& Son Ltd., Worcester and London.

Prayers about my friends

Dear Father God,
        Of all my friends
there's no one as important as you,
        no one who is as clever,
        no one who is as kind,
        no one who is as close,
because you are always with me
        – when I'm in the bath or in bed
        – when it's dark or all sunny and bright
        – when it's rainy or dry
        – when it's cold and snowy or boiling hot.
Thank you, God, because you are the best
        friend to have.
I know I can't see you but that doesn't matter,
        I know you're there.
I know you can hear me when I talk and that
        you understand just what I mean to
        say.

Thank you, Lord Jesus, for all my playgroup
    friends.
        Sometimes we play together in the
            sandpit or the Wendy House.
        Sometimes we play together in the
            painting corner or at the water tray.
Thank you for the friends who sit with me at
        dinner time
    and sit next to me at story time.
Thank you for my special friend . . .

Thank you, Lord, for my friends at Sunday
        School . . .
I only see them on Sundays
but I do like to sit with them at story time.
Thank you that I can learn about you with
        them and that we can paint pictures or
        act stories together.

Thank you, Lord, for my friends in our street.
I see them every day,
I play with them
    and sit to watch television with them.
Sometimes we go out together with our
        mums.
It is fun to live near my friends.

Sometimes my friends don't stay long.
One day they play;
    the next they want to fight.
One day they share;
    the next they snatch.
One day they give;
    the next they keep for themselves.
Mind you, Lord, I'm like that too;
    please help me not to be.

Thank you, Lord Jesus, because my friend is
       coming to stay.
She is coming for the night.
She will bring a case.
I'm so excited I feel like shouting.
I'm so happy.
I feel as if I can't wait till tomorrow
and I'll never sleep tonight.

Thank you, Lord Jesus, because I have a big
       friend.
He is much older than I am.
He shows me how to kick my ball
and use my cricket bat.
It is funny though,
when his big friends come out, he tells me to
       run away.
Why is it, God, you are so big, yet you always
       want me?

Dear Lord Jesus,
  Thank you for the friends I have made at
    my new school.
  They live a long way away from me.
  But we meet at school each day.
  One helps me take my coat off.
  One helps me with the buckles on my
    shoes.
  I help him tie his tie.
  (You see he can do buckles, I can't
  and I can do ties, he can't.)
Why can't we all be friends and help each
    other?
  Yes, and grown ups too?
  All the helping we could do –
  nobody would be lonely any more.

Prayers about my playtime

Dear Lord, thank you for making me so that I
     can pretend, and just for a few
     moments become another person –
     well nearly –
     a nurse in charge of a ward of patients,
     a garage mechanic running a big garage,
     a grown up lady looking after a house
     and family,
     a pilot flying an aeroplane.
Thank you because though you are God you
     did not just pretend to be like us. You
     really came as a little baby to our
     world.

Thank you, God, for Adventure Playgrounds
with their tunnels, their tyres,
     the little roads and houses,
     their special games.
Thank you for the people who first thought
     about them and planned them.
And thank you for all the people who build
     them and look after them.

Thank you, Father God, for the parks where I
        can play.
I can swing back and forward on the swings.
I can climb the stairs up the big slide
and come slipping down the shiny slide.
I can go up and down on the see-saw ever so
        high
and then ever so low.
I can throw a ball a very long way and run
        freely.
Thank you for green grass, for flower beds
        with their different coloured flowers,
        pink and red and yellow and purple
        and orange.
Parks are so big,
and I am so small.
Please always keep me safe.

Thank you, God, for all cuddly toys,
    my teddy bears, my dolls,
      and all the cuddly animals I can take to
        bed with me.
They are soft and furry.
They are good to feel and stroke.
They are good to feel against my cheek.
Thank you for all my soft cuddly toys.
Sometimes I don't want to let my friends play
      with them too.
Please help me not to be like that.

Thank you for the toys which help me learn,
    the dominoes which teach me to count,
    the plasticine which helps me to mould
      and model,
    the paint which helps me to use colours,
and the pencils with which I draw and write.
Thank you for jigsaw puzzles.
Thank you for toys which teach me.

I like to play with water and soap,
   I can blow bubbles,
   I can pour water from a jug or bottle.
I like to play with sand
   especially when it is a little bit wet.
   I like to fill a bucket and make a castle,
   I like to write with my finger on its
      smooth surface,
   I like to dig holes in it.
Thank you for sand and water, God.

Thank you, God,
   for stories which grown-ups read to me,
   for books with pictures and pages to turn
      over.
Thank you for rhymes,
   especially the ones where I use my
      fingers when I say them.
Thank you, God, for words, and sound.

Prayers about my special days

Lord Jesus,
Thank you for holidays when we go away.
I like to help with all the packing,
all sorts of piles of clothes,
    my shoes,
    my nightclothes,
    my skirts/trousers,
    my shorts and tee shirts.
And then we put them all into the big case,
    but it won't shut yet –
    so we sit on it
        and bounce
    until it is squeezed tight shut
        and locked.
Then Mummy packs the grown-ups' case for
      her and Daddy.
Thank you, God, for all the fun of packing.

Father God,
It is a lovely day today.
We are setting out on our holidays.
It is sunny and hot;
there isn't any breeze blowing;
there isn't a cloud in the sky.
I know some days it will sometimes rain;
the flowers need a drink
        – and so do we.
It would be nice if it would just rain
when I didn't want to go out.
But there are lots of other people in the world
        too, I know.
So thank you, God, for the sunshine and the
        rain too.

Dear Father God,
Thank you for sea and sand,
        for rocks and rambles,
        for pools and pebbles,
        for shells and swimming,
        for paddling and picnics.
I love the spray
and the foam,
the waves
and the splash.
Thank you for all the fun of the seaside.

I got lost on the beach today.
There were so many people who all looked
        the same.
There were so many children who all looked
        alike.
I felt like crying
        – in fact I did, a bit.
Still you took care of me.
        You always will,
        everywhere,
        at all times.
So thank you, God, even when I got lost, you
        looked after me and helped me find
        Mum and Dad.

Dear Father God,
I've been to the zoo today.
I saw lions with their golden manes,
elephants with their long grey trunks
and zebras with their stripes.
I saw monkeys leaping around, tails swinging
and giraffes with their thin legs and long,
            long necks.
I watched the seals flopping in and out of the
            water
and the kangaroos and wallabies as they
            hopped along the ground.
The animals looked just like the pictures in
            my book.
Thank you, God, for making all the animals
and for all the keepers who care for them in
            zoos and safari parks.

Thank you, God, for dentists.
I am going to see one today.
I am sure there will be other children waiting,
    looking at the comics in the waiting
        room,
wondering,
    wondering if I'm next or they are.
And then there's that funny chair,
it goes backwards
but it's comfy.
Fancy always looking into people's mouths
– that's what the dentist does.
He's kind and he has a little mirror to help
        him look.
I like him because he smiles at me.
He tells me to drink plenty of milk.
Thank you, God, for dentists who are so
        clever and for all good food to help my
        teeth to grow strong.

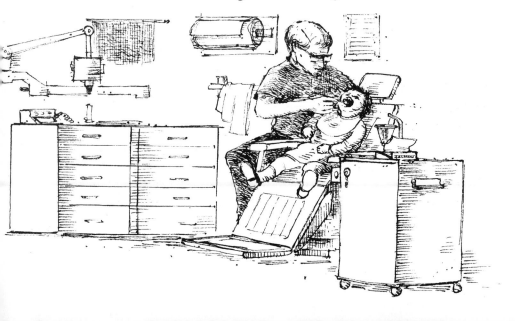

Thank you, God, for today.
    It is special –
I am going to nursery today
    for the very first time.
It will be different from home,
    in a bigger room
    with more windows and doors.
And there will be
    teachers
    and helpers
    and lots of other children.
I have got new shoes,
    new skirt/shorts,
    and a new tee shirt.
I think it's going to be fun,
    but I'm not sure.
I'm sure there will be lots of exciting things to
     do,
    new books,
    new paints,
    new toys and games.
And I know you are always with me
even in new adventures like this one.
Today is a very special day.
It's a new day,
    a new start.
Thank you, God, for my new nursery and all
     the fun I'm going to have there.

It is my birthday today.
I have so many cards –
    some have numbers on them,
    some have pictures of toys,
    some have pictures of flowers and birds,
    some have badges.
But they all wish me a happy day.
Thank you, God, for happy birthdays.

Oh, Lord Jesus, thank you for all my friends
and all the fun I shall have today.
Thank you for giving me strength to grow big
    and strong.
Daddy says he remembers when I was a new
    baby, how tiny I was;
what tiny feet,
what tiny hands I had.
Now it is my birthday and they remember
    when I was a baby –
Thank you, God.
Please keep me safe all through this year.

Dear Father God,
It's a special day today.
I have been waiting a long time for it.
I am going into hospital with Mum.
I shall see lots of nurses in their uniforms
and lots of doctors in white coats.
I have seen pictures in books
– in fact they sent me a special one
from the hospital to look at.
I still wonder what it's really going to be like;
what I shall feel like –
where Mum will be –
if it will hurt.
But thank you, God, you will be there with me
        all the time.

Prayers about my world

Lord Jesus, I have woken up and I don't feel
      very good.
My head is all heavy.
My eyes seem too full.
My legs ache and my arms feel so stiff.
Looking at my chest
    I see I've grown some big red splodges.
    I wonder what they are;
    ooh, they do itch
    and I do feel hot.
Please help the doctor to know what's the
      matter with me and give me nice
      tasting medicine to make me better.

Dear Lord Jesus,
It is clinic day today,
I am going with my mum.
It will smell funny — it always does —
    all clean and shiny.
It might be noisy — it often is —
babies will be laughing and crying,
and children will be calling out.
It may be crowded — it sometimes is —
    lots of different mums,
    lots of different children.
There might be lots of prams
    and buggies.
    and carrycots on wheels.
The doctors and nurses will want to look at
        me
to see how tall I am
    and how heavy.
They will give me bricks to build with
    and puzzles to do.
I'm glad we've got a clinic with kind nurses
        and doctors to help.

Thank you, Lord, for holidays, especially in
    the summer.
It is good to have Mummy and Daddy at
    home.
It is good to have treats.
It is good to go out for whole days.
It is good to be together as a family.
Thank you, God, for holidays.

Thank you, God, for picnics when we take our
    food outside.
Thank you for bags and baskets where we
    can pack our sandwiches and biscuits.
And for bottles of orange juice.
Thank you that everything tastes so good
    when we're out of doors.

Thank you, Lord Jesus, for the fun of going
      away.
I like to travel in a train –
the bustle of the station,
the screech of the brakes as the engine stops
      by the platform,
the banging of all the doors,
all the people calling goodbyes.
Thank you for trains.
I like to travel in cars –
the slamming of the doors which means
      we're safely shut in,
the engine purring as we travel along,
the breeze blowing against the roof rack,
and the wonderful feeling when we reach the
      journey's end.
Thank you for cars.

Thank you, God, for the postman.
I see him every morning.
He does the same thing every day,
    stops,
    sorts through his pile of letters,
    and then
    through the box it comes,
    and plop on the mat.
Daddy doesn't like the bills
and Mummy doesn't either.
I like Grannie's letters
and the picture postcards.
Thank you for postmen.
Please keep them safe as they go on their
    rounds.

I do like ice-creams,
especially on a hot sunny day:
    wafers,
    cones
    and lollies too.
I know when he comes by the tune he plays
– Mummy says it isn't a tune at all.
I like giving the ice-cream man my money,
especially when I get some back.
Sometimes when there's a lot of traffic about
it's difficult to get to the ice-cream van.
Please help me to be careful even when I
      want to hurry.
Thank you for ice-cream vans and for all the
      ice-creams and lollies.

Thank you, God, for television.
I enjoy watching it with Mummy.
I wonder sometimes how it works.
When the man comes to mend it
it looks so strange when he takes the
back off:
lots of knobs,
lots of wires
and nuts
and bolts.
Thank you, God.

Prayers about me and God

I am going to church today,
    it's Sunday,
    God's special day.
Church is big,
it smells different from home somehow
    – lots of furniture polish and flowers.
It's high and lofty,
the seats are wooden, and a long way from
      the floor.
My legs and feet dangle,
    I can swing them back and forwards.
I wonder if God likes his house
because that's what some people call the
      church.
I wonder if he likes his family
because that's what Mummy says we are.
I do hope I shall learn more about him,
    as I grow up
    and come to church more.

Dear Lord Jesus,
What is heaven like?
I would like to know.
Mummy says we don't really know
       – even grown-ups.
But you are there –
there isn't any crying there.
And I am so glad since I don't like listening to
       crying.
There isn't any hurt there either.
And I am so glad of that too, since I don't like
       being hurt either.
There isn't any dark there
and that's good because I like the daylight.
So I think I'm going to like heaven anyway.

Lord Jesus,
It's Easter today.
We've had a sad day on Friday,
when we thought about you on a cross.
But now everyone is happy because you are
        alive;
you will never die again.
We are going to church today,
to show how happy we are that you are alive.
We shall say to everyone, 'Be happy, Jesus is
        alive!'
Everyone will say to us, 'Be happy, Jesus is
        alive!'
Thank you for all you did for us,
    dying on the cross.
Thank you for being alive again;
    we are so happy today.

Dear Father God,
it's harvest,
the church is full of people.
There are rosy apples,
yellow bananas, smooth pears;
there are rough potatoes,
long green beans, fat cabbages, round
        cauliflowers;
there are heavy tins,
thin packets and polished jars;
there are flowers everywhere, orange, red,
        yellow and white.
We are coming to thank you for all the good
        things you give us and to share with
        some people who haven't as much as
        we have.

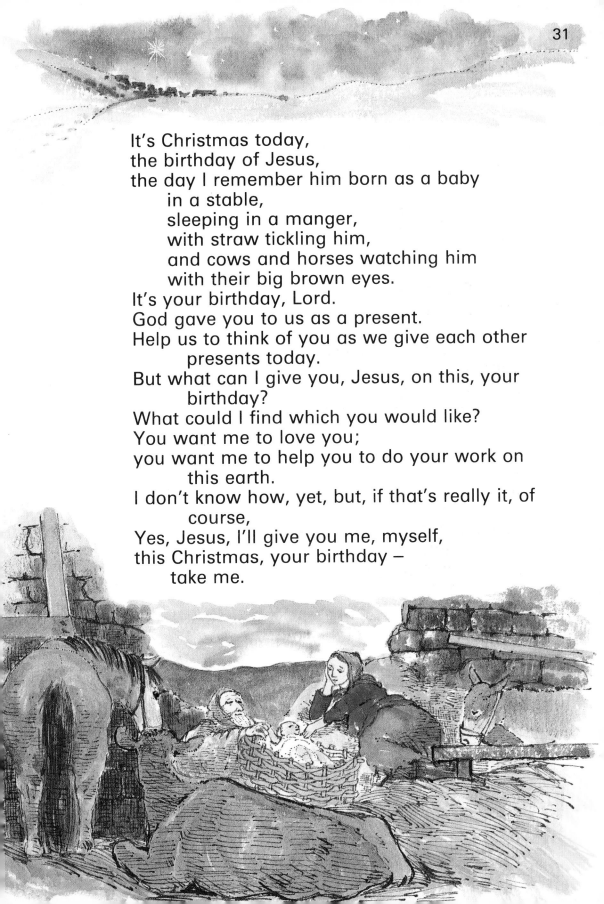

It's Christmas today,
the birthday of Jesus,
the day I remember him born as a baby
    in a stable,
      sleeping in a manger,
      with straw tickling him,
      and cows and horses watching him
      with their big brown eyes.
It's your birthday, Lord.
God gave you to us as a present.
Help us to think of you as we give each other
      presents today.
But what can I give you, Jesus, on this, your
      birthday?
What could I find which you would like?
You want me to love you;
you want me to help you to do your work on
      this earth.
I don't know how, yet, but, if that's really it, of
      course,
Yes, Jesus, I'll give you me, myself,
this Christmas, your birthday –
    take me.

Dear Lord Jesus,
    I know I want to help you,
    I know I want you to be my friend,
but I find it hard
    sometimes
to be obedient to grown-ups,
    not to lose my temper
    and always to be kind.
Still, I know from church,
    from my Sunday School teacher
    that you love me
    and that you can help me,
    – please do!

Dear Father God,
I want to talk to you in my own words,
as if you were right here by me,
And that's where you are.
You are with me;
thank you for listening in while I talk.